ENERGY FOR THE FUTURE AND GLOBAL WARMING

BIOFUELS

By Andrew Solway

Consultant: Suzy Gazlay, M.A.,
science curriculum resource teacher

Gareth Stevens
Publishing

Please visit our web site at: www.garethstevens.com
For a free color catalog describing Gareth Stevens Publishing's
list of high-quality books, call 1-800-542-2595 (USA) or
1-800-387-3178 (Canada).
Gareth Stevens Publishing fax: 1-877-542-2596

Library of Congress Cataloging-in-Publication Data

Solway, Andrew.
  Biofuels / Andrew Solway.
    p. cm. — (Energy for the future and global warming)
  Includes index.
  ISBN-10: 0-8368-8398-5   ISBN-13: 978-0-8368-8398-5 (lib. bdg.)
  ISBN-10: 0-8368-8407-8   ISBN-13: 978-0-8368-8407-4 (softcover)
  1. Biomass energy—Juvenile literature. I. Title.
TP339.S65   2008
662'.88—dc22   2007008748

This edition first published in 2008 by
Gareth Stevens Publishing
A Weekly Reader® Company
1 Reader's Digest Road
Pleasantville, NY 10570-7000 USA

Copyright © 2008 by Gareth Stevens, Inc.

Produced by Discovery Books
Editors: Geoff Barker and Sabrina Crewe
Designer: Keith Williams
Photo researcher: Rachel Tisdale
Illustrations: Stefan Chabluk and Keith Williams

Gareth Stevens editor: Carol Ryback
Gareth Stevens art direction and design: Tammy West
Gareth Stevens production: Jessica Yanke

Photo credits: www.greasecar.com: / Kathy Tarantola cover, title page, 21.
U.S. Department of Agriculture: / Scott Bauer 8, 17; / Keith Weller 27.
Practical Action: / Zul 10. DOE / NREL: / Richard Bain 13; / Warren Gretz 22.
Svensk Biogas: 15; / Lasse Hejdenberg 18. U.S. DOE / National Energy Technology
Laboratory: 23. DONG Energy: 24.

Printed in the United States of America

4 5 6 7 8 9 11 10 09 08

CONTENTS

Cover photo: Justin Carven, owner of Greasecar Vegetable Fuel Systems of Florence, Massachusetts, designed a fuel conversion kit. Carven's kit allows diesel engine vehicles to also run on used cooking oil.

Words in **boldface** appear in the glossary or in the "Key Words" boxes within the chapters.

CHAPTER ONE

ENERGY AND GLOBAL WARMING

Every day, people at home and at work are using energy. A huge amount of energy goes into heating and lighting homes and other buildings. Even when we are sleeping, we are using energy. Many electronics and appliances in the home are consuming lots of power even when we are not using them.

People use a lot of energy to travel around. About 28 percent of the energy used in the United States is for transporting people and goods. Forty percent of

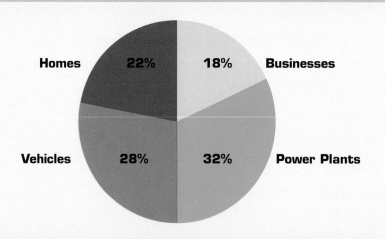

ENERGY USE IN THE UNITED STATES IN 2005

Homes 22%   18% Businesses

Vehicles 28%   32% Power Plants

This chart shows energy use in the United States. It shows how much was used by homes, businesses, **power plants**, and vehicles.

WHAT IS ENERGY?

Energy gives us the power we use to do things. It comes in different forms. Heat is a form of energy. We can use it to warm buildings, cook food, and run machines. We get heat from burning fossil fuels. A fossil fuel is a primary (first) source of energy. A secondary source of energy is produced by the burning of a primary energy source. For instance, electricity is our main secondary source of energy. We make electricity from fossil fuels or from the power of moving water. We can even make electricity from solar energy (the energy in sunlight).

our energy is used in homes and businesses.

The world gets more than 85 percent of its energy from oil, coal, and natural gas. These are **fossil fuels**. We burn fossil fuels to run the furnaces that heat our homes. Vehicle engines and airplane engines run on fossil fuels. Most of the electricity we use is made in power plants that burn fossil fuels.

The demand for more

The world's population keeps growing. Today, there are almost three times as many people as there were fifty years ago. All these people need energy to live.

When we need more energy, we use more fossil fuels. We cannot keep doing this forever. Fossil fuels are not **renewable**. We cannot make more fossil fuels once supplies run out.

Fossil fuel problems

There are other problems with fossil fuels, too. When we burn fossil fuels, they produce smoke and harmful gases. The smoke from fossil fuels can cause smog. Smog is a type of chemical fog that affects the quality of the air we breathe.

Chemicals, such as sulfur, from the waste gases make rain, sleet, and snow harmful when they fall to Earth. This is called **acid rain**. Acid rain kills fish in lakes and rivers. Acid rain also damages plant life and buildings.

Global warming

Waste gases from fossil fuels build up in the atmosphere. They let heat from the Sun reach Earth, but they do not let any extra heat rise back into space. We call these **greenhouse gases** because they trap heat much like the walls and roof of a greenhouse.

Carbon dioxide is one of the main greenhouse gases from fossil fuels. Water vapor and **methane** are two other greenhouse gases. These gases help keep Earth warm enough for life to exist. But too many greenhouse gases put the world's climate out of balance.

Burning fossil fuels in large amounts adds more greenhouse gases into the air than normal. The average amounts of greenhouse gases in the air have increased in the last hundred years. Scientists believe this increase is causing Earth to get warmer than it should be. This changes the worldwide weather patterns, or climate. The climate change is called **global warming**.

Biofuels

We need to reduce the rate of global warming. The best way to do this is to use fewer fossil fuels. This will lower the amounts of greenhouse gases going into the air.

One way to cut the use of fossil fuels is to replace them with biofuels. A biofuel is fuel made from **biomass** (material from plants or animals). Wood is the most common biofuel. Used cooking oil or leftover plant products from crops, such as corn, can be used as biofuel. Even trash can become a biofuel! Like other fuels, biofuels store energy.

THE CARBON CYCLE

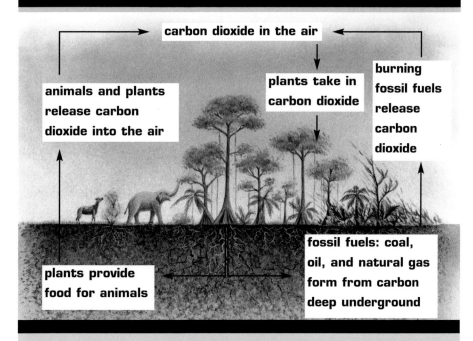

carbon dioxide in the air

animals and plants release carbon dioxide into the air

plants take in carbon dioxide

burning fossil fuels release carbon dioxide

plants provide food for animals

fossil fuels: coal, oil, and natural gas form from carbon deep underground

Carbon is reused in a constant cycle. For example, during its lifetime, a tree removes tons of carbon dioxide from the air. When trees (or fossil fuels) are burned, carbon dioxide is released back into the air.

EFFECTS OF GLOBAL WARMING

Global warming affects all of Earth. Rising temperatures are causing the ice caps at the North and South Poles to melt. As ice melts into the sea, and sea levels rise. High sea levels mean that floods happen more often. Some low-lying places may soon be permanently flooded. Other areas get less rain because of global warming. Some of these places may become deserts. Food crops may fail. Many kinds of plants and animals may die out because the places where they live will become too hot or too dry.

A research station in this Idaho valley records the dates that snow cover on the mountains begins to melt each year. Scientists have predicted that global warming will cause the snow to melt earlier every year. Shorter snowfall seasons mean less water for surrounding farmlands.

Renewable and clean

Biofuels are renewable. If you cut down a tree and burn it for fuel, you can also plant a new tree to eventually replace the wood you burned.

When wood burns, it produces carbon dioxide,

BIOFUELS

GOOD THINGS	PROBLEMS
Renewable	Large areas of land needed to grow plant material for making biofuels
Can replace fossil fuels with only small changes to engines and furnaces	Often does not produce as much energy as the same amount of fossil fuels
Can be made from materials that would otherwise become waste	Crops grown just for biofuels use up energy, usually in the form of fossil fuels
When burned, produce fewer polluting gases and carbon dioxide than fossil fuels	Using food crops to make biofuels could cause higher food prices and food shortages

just as fossil fuels do. But plants capture carbon dioxide as they grow. Every day a plant is alive, it absorbs (takes in) carbon dioxide from the air. The carbon dioxide released during wood burning nearly balances the carbon dioxide the tree absorbed during its lifetime. It does not add to greenhouse gases and global warming as much as fossil fuels do.

KEY WORDS

biomass: any kind of material that comes from animals or plants
fossil fuels: fuels formed in the ground over millions of years, including coal, oil, and natural gas
greenhouse gases: gases in the atmosphere that trap heat energy
renewable: having a new or reusable supply of material constantly available

CHAPTER TWO

LOOKING AT BIOFUELS

Biofuels, such as wood, charcoal, and dried manure (animal waste), have been used as fuels for thousands of years. In the past, biofuels were used for lighting rooms and other areas. Plant oils and animal fats were used as fuel for oil lamps. Biofuels can also be burned to produce heat on open fires or in stoves. Stoves are more **efficient** than open fires. They turn more of the stored energy in the fuel into heat. Modern wood-burning

The Practical Action organization has helped many people in Bangladesh make improved cooking stoves. Made from clay and a metal grill, these stoves use about half the fuel of regular stoves.

RUDOLPH DIESEL (1858-1913)

Rudolph Diesel was a German engineer who invented the diesel engine. He thought of developing a diesel engine in the early 1890s. In 1893, Diesel built his first test engine. It exploded and nearly killed him. He kept improving his design. By 1897, he had an engine that worked well. By 1898, Diesel was selling his engines. They sold very well, and he was soon a millionaire.

stoves burn less fuel than an open fire, and they produce less ash.

Biofuel engines

Some of the earliest engines ran on biofuels. The first diesel engines, made in about 1897, ran on peanut oil. Diesel engines compress (squash) air and fuel. As the mixture gets compressed, it get hotter and starts to burn. Fuels made with vegetable fat or oil, such as peanut oil, are called **biodiesel**.

In the early 1900s, the first Ford automobiles ran on a biofuel called **ethanol**. This type of biofuel is an alcohol made from plant sugars. Ethanol can be made from grains such as wheat and rice. It can even be made from grass clippings.

In 1901, huge amounts of petroleum (oil) were found in Texas. Within a few years, oil companies were producing very cheap gasoline and diesel fuels. These fossil fuels gradually replaced biofuels.

Ethanol

Today, scientists are still working on developing good biofuels. Ethanol is produced for vehicle fuel. To make ethanol, plant material is mixed with yeast and kept warm. Yeast is a single-celled organism that feeds on plant material. The yeast turns sugars into alcohol. This process is called **fermentation**.

In the United States, ethanol is usually made from corn. It is mixed with the gasoline we put in our vehicles. Ethanol is not as good a fuel as gasoline. It produces about one-third less energy than the same amount of gasoline. But it produces fewer polluting gases. Blending 10 percent ethanol with 90 percent gasoline helps reduce **pollution**.

Brazil is the world's largest ethanol producer. Brazil makes its ethanol from sugarcane. The sugarcane is crushed to remove the sugar. The sugar is then fermented. Many cars and other vehicles in Brazil run on a mix of 25 percent ethanol and 75 percent gasoline.

"Making ethanol is already half as cheap as making gasoline. Researchers at Argonne and around the nation are investigating ways to create new bioproducts [fuels from biomass] that can compete with petrochemicals [fuels from oil] on cost and performance."

Seth Snyder, biochemical engineer and the leader of the Chemical and Biotechnology Section in Argonne National Laboratory's Energy Systems Division, Argonne, Illinois, 2006

Seven percent of Hawaii's electricity is made by burning bagasse, or sugarcane waste (the mound in the center of the photograph). Since 2006, Hawaii has been making ethanol from the sugarcane itself.

The remains of the sugarcane after it has been crushed is called bagasse. Dried bagasse is also used as a fuel. It can be burned in a power plant to make electricity. Sugarcane can provide both the sugar to make ethanol and the power needed to keep the ethanol factory running.

Biodiesel

Vegetable oil can be used as a biodiesel, just like the peanut oil in the first diesel engines. Today's biodiesels, however, are blended to help them work better. They are made with vegetable oil and an alcohol, such as ethanol. The fuel produced is thinner

13

"Best of all, biodiesel feedstock sources are renewable and can be produced locally. While fossil fuels formed over millions of years (and are being rapidly depleted), biodiesel can be created in just a few months."

Greg Pahl, author of the book, *Biodiesel: Growing a New Energy Economy* (2005)

than vegetable oil, and it burns more efficiently.

Biodiesel can be made from many kinds of oil. Soybean oil is the most common, but palm oil and other oils are used, too. Biodiesel can also be made from waste cooking oil and from animal fats.

Biodiesel produces less pollution than regular diesel made from petroleum. It is much less toxic (poisonous), too. Biodiesel is also biodegradable, which means it can break down and become part of the soil without causing harm.

Biodiesel fuel can be mixed with regular diesel fuel without harming a standard diesel engine. Diesel fuel is still needed to start the vehicle and shut it down, however. Carmakers often will not guarantee an engine that an owner adapts (changes) to use biodiesel.

Biogas

As its name shows, **biogas** is a gas rather than a liquid. Ethanol is made by using yeast to ferment plant sugars. Biogas is made by fermenting plant or animal material in a closed container. Instead of yeast,

The biogas plant in Linkoping, Sweden, produces methane from a mixture of organic waste. The waste is heated in special tanks, forming the gases methane and carbon dioxide. The biogas is then cleaned of the carbon dioxide to leave pure methane fuel.

the process uses **bacteria,** tiny life-forms made of only one cell.

The great advantage of biogas is that it can be made from all kinds of matter. Sewage (waste and wastewater from homes and other buildings) can be turned into biogas. Rotting trash gives off biogas. It can be collected at large dumps and landfills (places where trash is buried in the ground).

GROWING SPACE

There is a big question about biodiesel. Soybeans and other plants must be grown to make vegetable oil. Growing soybeans or other crops takes up a lot of land. Making enough biodiesel to supply the United States would take all the country's farmland.

If biodiesel is going to replace fossil fuels in the future, we will need to find a better way to produce it. One method uses **algae**. Algae are very tiny water plants. The green scum on the surface of a pond is one kind of algae. Scientists have discovered that biodiesel can be made from certain fast-growing algae with high oil content.

Growing algae would take up a lot less space than soybeans and other crops. Algae can grow in shallow pools of water on land that is not used for anything else. Just 1 acre (0.4 hectares) of land would hold enough algae to make 15,000 gallons (57,000 liters) of biodiesel. Scientists estimate that less than 10 million acres (4 million hectares) of algae-growing land would produce enough biodiesel for all the transportation fuel needed by the United States. In 2006, nearly 80 million acres (32 million hectares) of U.S. farmland was used just for growing corn.

The hairy pod of a soybean contains two to four seeds. Soybean seeds are processed to produce soybean oil. Soybeans have many uses, including vegetable oil for cooking, cosmetics, plastics, and biodiesel.

In Japan, seaweed is taken from the seashore and used to make biogas.

The main fuel in biogas is methane. Biogas also contains other gases. The methane

BIOGAS CITY

The city of Linkoping, Sweden, uses a lot of biogas. Linkoping's biogas is made by fermenting offal (waste animal parts). All the buses in Linkoping run on biogas. The taxis and garbage trucks use biogas, too. The world's first biogas train runs out of Linkoping as well.

Amanda is one of sixty-five trains in Linkoping, Sweden, that run on biogas. The biogas is made from fermented offal. Inedible material from the body of one cow will power the train for about 2.5 miles (4 kilometers).

needs to be separated from these gases before it can be used as a fuel. Once it has been purified, biogas can be used in the same way as natural gas. It can be used to make electricity or to power vehicles.

The country of Sri Lanka gets 45 percent of its energy from biogas. The gas is produced on a small scale. Farmers use a tank called a digester to make methane from animal manure. The methane is used for cooking and to produce electricity. Whatever is left in the tank is used as a fertilizer on fields.

Butanol

A substance called butanol is another future biofuel. Butanol is an alcohol, like ethanol. It is made using a kind of bacteria. These bacteria can make butanol from wood and all kinds of biomass (plant material). The bacteria act like yeast to digest, or ferment, plant material. The process separates the biomass into

layers. Then the butanol can be removed.

Butanol produces more energy than ethanol. Some people use butanol instead of gasoline in their cars. Carmakers warn this may damage the engine.

KEY WORDS

bacteria: tiny life-forms made of only one cell
biodiesel: a fuel, made from plant oil, that is used in diesel engines
biogas: a fuel made by fermenting plant or animal matter. Biogas is similar to natural gas and consists mostly of methane.
ethanol: a form of alcohol made from plant sugars that is used as a biofuel
fermentation: a series of chemical reactions that convert sugars to alcohol or gas. The reactions are caused by yeast or bacteria feeding on the sugars.

CHAPTER THREE

USING BIOFUELS

Biofuels supply only a very small amount of the world's energy. This is beginning to change. Around the world, more people are interested in using biofuels.

Biofuels can directly replace fossil fuels. They produce less carbon dioxide and other polluting gases. There are questions that need answering, however.

- There are many different biofuels. Which ones are best for which jobs?
- The way biofuels are made is also important. What is the cleanest way to make biodiesel?
- What about cost? Can we make biofuels cheap enough that people can afford to use them?

In this chapter, we will look at ways biofuels are being used around the world. This will help us understand how we may use biofuels in the future.

Biofuel for vehicles

Of all energy sources, biofuels offer the best hope for reducing the amount of carbon dioxide waste produced by vehicles. Most cars currently in use could run on a mixture of biofuel and fossil fuels. Many countries already use biofuels in their vehicles. Some gas stations sell mixtures of gasoline and ethanol. Other gas stations also offer regular diesel mixed with biodiesel.

THE GREASECAR

In 1998, Justin Carven was a student at Hampshire College, in Amherst, Massachusetts. He began developing a system to run his car on used cooking oil. Eight years later, he had a large factory making fuel conversion kits that allow cars to run on cooking oil.

Vehicles using the Greasecar Vegetable Fuel System have two tanks — one for used cooking oil and one for diesel. The diesel is used to heat the oil. It is also used for starting and shutting down the engine.

The Greasecar kit costs about $800, but it saves drivers thousands of dollars. Most of Carven's customers get their used cooking oil for free from restaurants. The restaurants are happy to get rid of it! In 2006, one trucker told a national TV news program that he saved $400 to $600 a week on fuel for his truck.

In 2006, Justin Carven sold about three thousand fuel conversion kits to people who wanted to recycle used cooking oil to run their cars.

In the future, more power plants may use wood chips (above) and other biofuels to produce power for homes and businesses.

Making electricity

Biofuels are also used to make electricity. An electric **power plant** burns fuel in a furnace to heat water until it turns into steam. A jet of hot steam is fed into a machine called a **turbine**. Inside the turbine, the steam's power pushes and turns large blades. The motion turns a **generator**, a machine that makes electricity.

Most power plants today burn fossil fuels. But biofuels can be used instead. Biodiesel, biogas, bagasse (sugarcane waste), and woodchips can fuel power plants. Today, a few small power plants use biofuels. In some larger power plants, biofuels are mixed with fossil fuels.

Combined cycle

Power plants that work using steam turbines are not very

The Wabash River Coal Gasification Repowering Project is the first full-size commercial gasification-combined cycle plant built in the United States. Located outside West Terre Haute, Indiana, the plant started full operations in November 1995.

efficient. They turn less than 30 percent of the energy produced by the fuel into electricity. The rest is lost as heat. Some new power plants, called combined-cycle power plants, are much more efficient. They turn nearly 60 percent of the fuel energy into electricity.

In combined-cycle power plants, a jet of hot natural gas is used to turn the blades of a turbine that powers a generator. The turbine gives off hot waste gas in the process. This waste gas heats water and makes steam. The steam powers another turbine, which turns another generator. The same gas is used twice!

Natural gas is a fossil fuel. It is nonrenewable. Biogas is renewable. It is

BIOPOWER

Some power plants use a system known as combined heat and power (CHP). The heat produced by making electrical power is captured instead of wasted. The heat is sent through pipes to warm buildings in nearby cities.

In Denmark, all new power plants must use CHP. Avedore 2 in Copenhagen, Denmark, burns leftover wood from a flooring business. It also burns straw. (The ash from the straw is returned to the growing fields for use as fertilizer.) Avedore 2 generates enough electricity for about 800,000 homes. It supplies heat for approximately 110,000 homes. Avedore 2 is also one of the cleanest power plants in the world.

Avedore 2 power plant in Denmark opened in 2001. Its combined heat and power plant system makes it one of the cleanest power plants in the world.

ELECTRICITY FROM SEAWEED

Japanese researchers are testing a method for making electricity from seaweed. The seaweed is fermented to make biogas. The gas is used to power an electricity generator in a small power plant. It produces enough electricity for about twenty houses. If the tests work well, a much larger power plant will be built.

almost identical to natural gas. Both biogas and natural gas consist mostly of methane. If we can produce enough biogas economically, it can replace natural gas in combined-cycle power plants.

There are some problems with producing biofuels. Today's biodiesel and ethanol biofuels are made from food crops. It takes a lot of energy to grow these crops. Biofuel crops include sugarcane, corn, and soybeans. They must be grown on good farmland. The crops have to be planted and harvested. They also need fertilizers and weed killers. These materials can cause pollution.

KEY WORDS

generator: a machine that uses mechanical energy to make electricity
power plant: a factory that produces electricity
turbine: a type of engine powered by a flow of fluid, such as air, steam, or water. Turbines have large blades that spin, creating energy that powers an electric generator.

CHAPTER FOUR

FUEL FOR THE FUTURE

Worldwide use of biofuels is growing fast. The first stages for changing to biofuel are already in place. Gas stations in Brazil have been selling a mixture of gasoline and ethanol for many years. Gas stations in the United States are now selling this kind of fuel, too. In England and Europe, biodiesel is more popular than bioethanol.

The next stage

Biofuel still costs more to make on a large scale than ordinary fuel. In some countries, including Germany and Sweden, the government

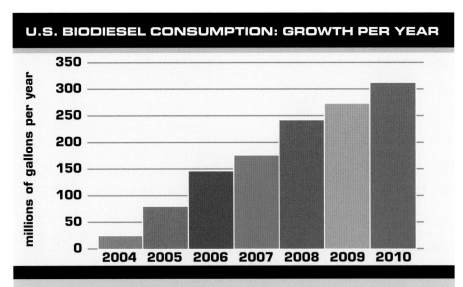

U.S. BIODIESEL CONSUMPTION: GROWTH PER YEAR

millions of gallons per year

U.S. biodiesel consumption (use) could grow to 300 million gallons (1.1 billion liters) per year by 2010.

Scientists are experimenting with alfalfa and other plants. They are studying the efficiency of converting such common plants into biofuels.

gives money to biofuel companies. This helps keep fuel prices down for people who want to buy biofuels.

Cost is not the only issue. To make more use of biofuels, car engines must change. We need engines that can run on pure biofuel. Carmakers are already producing test cars that can do this.

Biofuels can also be used for other vehicles. Most ships are powered by large diesel engines. These could be converted to work with biodiesel quite easily.

Aircraft biofuel has been harder to make. Aircraft fuel sometimes needs to work at very low temperatures. Most biofuels turns into solids at low temperatures. Scientists are developing biofuels that stay liquid when blended with regular aircraft fuel.

Making enough

Biofuel mixtures will be used in power plants of the future. These power plants will require huge amounts of fuel. If we want to use more biofuels, we need to produce more, too. There is a limit to how much biofuel can be produced from crops such as corn, sugarcane, and soybeans. We will need to produce biofuels from other materials, too. Tough, woody plants — such as some wild grasses — need much less energy to grow. But these kinds of plants are harder to turn into biofuel, so they cost more to process.

Producing biodiesel from algae will also help increase the supply of biofuel. Using different types of **waste** for biofuel will also give us a source of clean energy. At the

ALGAE: TWICE AS USEFUL

In the near future, we may be able to cut power plant **emissions** (waste gases) even more. U.S. researchers are experimenting with growing algae in the chimneys of power plants. The algae absorb (take in) carbon dioxide and other gases from the smoke going up the chimney. The algae reduce the carbon dioxide emissions by 40 percent. The algae, meanwhile, use these gases to grow very fast. Every day, some of the algae can be harvested (collected) and turned into biodiesel. That way, the algae can reduce carbon dioxide emissions and make new fuel at the same time.

same time, it will help reduce waste gases and trash.

Microbes

Biofuels are made from food crops, grasses, wood, algae, garbage, sewage, offal (waste animal parts), and manure. **Microbes** — very tiny plants or animals, such as yeast and bacteria — are already used to make many biofuels. In the future, microbes will offer even more ways to produce biofuels. Specially developed microbes may make biofuels from other materials, even waste plastic.

What's the future?

The Bush administration has proposed an energy goal for the future. By 2025, about 25 percent of available energy in the U.S. must be manufactured from agricultural resources.

It is unlikely, however, that biofuels alone will completely replace fossil fuels. It is more realistic to consider biofuel as one of several sources of renewable energy. Wind power, solar energy (energy from sunlight), geothermal energy (heat from the ground), and water power will also be widely used. Still, biofuels will undoubtedly play an important role in our future energy needs.

KEY WORDS

emissions: (usually) polluting substances that are given off during power production
microbes: tiny plants or animals that cannot be seen without a microscope
waste: unused by-product — extra materials left over that are not needed or that cause pollution

GLOSSARY

acid rain: any precipitation that is too acidic (polluted)

algae: usually tiny, plant-like water-based life-forms

bacteria: tiny life-forms with only one cell

biodiesel: a fuel made from plant oil that can be used in diesel engines

biogas: a fuel made by fermenting plant or animal matter. Biogas is similar to natural gas and consists mostly of methane.

biomass: any kind of material that comes from animals or plants

efficient: working well and without much waste

ethanol: a form of alcohol made from plant sugars that is used as a biofuel

fermentation: a series of chemical reactions caused by yeast or bacteria that convert sugars to alcohol or gas

generator: a machine that changes mechanical energy into electricity

global warming: the gradual warming of Earth's climate

greenhouse gases: gases in the atmosphere that trap heat energy

methane: one of the gases found in natural gas; also given off by biomass as it decays

pollution: the process of making land, air, or water impure or dirty with waste gases or other substances

power plant: a factory that produces electricity

renewable: having a new or reusable supply of material constantly available

turbine: a type of engine powered by a flow of fluid. Turbines have large spinning blades that spin a shaft to power a generator.

The following list highlights the major fuel sources of the twenty-first century. It also lists some advantages and disadvantages of each:

	Advantages	Disadvantages
Biofuels	renewable energy source; widely available from a number of sources, including farms, restaurants, and everday garbage	fossil fuels often used to grow farm crops; requires special processing facilities that run on fossil fuels in order to produce usable biofuel
Fossil fuels: coal, oil, petroleum	used by functioning power plants worldwide; supports economies	limited supplies; emit greenhouse gases; produce toxic wastes; must often be transported long distances
Geothermal energy	nonpolluting; renewable; free source	only available in localized areas; would require redesign of heating systems
Hydrogen (fuel cells)	most abundant element in the universe; nonpolluting	fuel cell production uses up fossil fuels; hydrogen gas storage presents safety issues
Nuclear energy	produces no greenhouse gases; produces a lot of energy from small amounts of fuel	solid wastes remain dangerous for centuries; limited life span of power plants
Solar power	renewable; produces no pollutants; free source	weather and climate dependent; solar cells expensive to manufacture
Water power	renewable resource; generally requires no additional fuel	requires flowing water, waves, or tides; can interfere with view; dams may destroy large natural areas and disrupt human settlements
Wind power	renewable; nonpolluting; free source	depends on weather patterns; depends on location; endangers bird populations

RESOURCES

Books

Morris, Neil.
Biomass Power.
Energy Sources (series).
Smart Apple Media (2006)

Povey, Karen D.
Biofuels.
Our Environment (series).
KidHaven Press (2006)

Web Site

www.eia.doe.gov/kids/energyfacts/ sources/renewable/biomass.html
Visit the U.S. Department of Energy's Web site describing the different kinds of biofuels.

Publisher's note to educators and parents: Our editors have carefully reviewed these Web sites to ensure that they are suitable for children. Many Web sites change frequently, however, and we cannot guarantee that a site's future contents will continue to meet our high standards of quality and educational value. Be advised that children should be closely supervised whenever they access the Internet.

INDEX